Soulfie

Set your soul free

Lillian Khan

IOWI

Copyright © 2017 Lillian Khan. All Rights Reserved.

No part of this book may be reproduced in whole or in part, in any form, or stored on any device including digital media, except with the prior written permission of the author. Exceptions are granted for brief quotations utilized in critical articles or reviews with due credit given to the author.

For more information on the author/her works visit:
www.soulpoetess.com
email: soulpoetesslillian@gmail.com

ISBN: 978-1-926926-87-2

Cover illustration:
Yosha Khan

Published by:
In Our Words Inc.
inourwords.ca
inourwords2008@gmail.com
251 Queen Street South, Suite #561,
Streetsville, ON L5M 1L7

"Music in the soul can be heard by the universe."
~ *Lao Tzu*

Dedication

For my children,
Yosha, Yohannah, Juwairiya, Ukasha and Aliya,
whom I love with all my heart

Why Soulfie?

A tidal wave of selfies,
drowning us all in external superficialities...

Going deeper than the superficial,
avoiding the hype of this social ritual...

It is time for authenticity
Set the soul free!
Take a soulfie!

excerpt from the poem Soulfie

Contents

A Graceful Age 1
A Letter to Death 2
A Requiem for Asha 3
And the Angels cried 4
Assumptions and Presumptions 6
At the End of the Day 8
Be Gentle with Yourself 9
Be Selective 10
Be You 12
Begin Again 13
Beyond 14
Breath 15
Broken Mirror 16
Can You Miss Someone You Never Met? 17
Childless 18
Common Enchantment 19
Cyber Fantasy 20
Dance with the Universe 21
Death, I am not Happy with You 22
Disillusioned 23
Does She Love You Like I Did? 24
Don't 25
Don't Chase After People 26
Exquisite Paradox 27
Flashback 28
Freedom of Speech 29
Gender Bender 30
Gone Without a Trace 32
Grandma's House 33

Grief 34
Her Darkness 35
I Thank You 36
If We Could Live Our Lives Backwards 37
In My Lifetime 38
Inferno 39
It Makes Me Sad 40
Just a Housewife 41
Let Them Fly 42
Letters to My Children 44
Letting Go 46
Loss 47
Minefields 48
Misfit 49
My Heart Lies in Mumbai 50
Not Missed 51
Ode to Curry 52
Old Pictures 53
On the Subway 54
Practice 55
Prisoner of My Mind 56
Progeny 58
Pump Up Your Faith 59
Raw 60
Refugee 61
Rise Above Judgment 62
Soulfie 63
Sex Sold 64
She Bled Quietly 65
She Dreamed of Being a Princess 66
She Stood her Ground 67

Silence	68
Sitting at My Window	69
Slow Death	70
So What?	71
Sorry to Disappoint You	72
Stay With Me	73
Stress	74
Suicide	75
The Ache	76
The Beggar	77
The Bus Journey	78
The Dance	79
The Flower	80
The Garden of the Soul	81
The Hunter and the Hunted	82
The Little Girl Inside	83
The Old Itch	84
The Shirt	85
The Trial	86
The Unicorn, the Fairy, the Mermaid, the Clown	87
Today	88
You are Beautiful	89
Vigilant	90
Walls	91
War	92
We are all One	93
What am I?	94
Wouldn't You Rather Just be Ordinary?	96
Acknowledgements	98

A Graceful Age

Have you ever watched a tree...
seen how it ages so gracefully,
through winter, summer, spring and fall,
even when all it's leaves fall...
It stands so strong and so bold,
through extreme heat and biting cold.
The four seasons come and leave their mark,
but the tree never loses it's spark...
It's leaves turn green, then orange and gold,
a never-ending tale repeatedly told...
It stands tall, through storms and squalls,
with resilience it weathers it all...
Even when winter lays her bare,
she wears her nakedness with so much flair.
Would that we could be like this,
it would be serenity, sheer bliss!
Let's take a leaf from a tree today,
she really knows how to lead the way...
She trusts the maker and her destiny,
and knows how to age gracefully!

A Letter to Death

I am not ready, spare me this round...
Check me out, the next time around.
I still have, so much to do...
don't want to leave stuff undone
to regret and rue.
Lovers to love, new friends to befriend...
Family to love, unconditionally till the end.
Please give me, just one more day,
I still have so much to say!

A Requiem for Asha

I got the sad news that Asha,
the lady who worked tirelessly in my home,
sweeping, cleaning, washing clothes, mopping the floor, is no more...
Ironically her name, Asha, meant 'hope'...
But poverty squeezed the joy from her life,
it was around her neck like a rope...

She lived her life like a fierce warrior,
meeting her battles head on,
in the midst of dire poverty and squalor.
Generations of her ancestors,
were caught in the vicious cycle of poverty,
yet defiance to her living conditions,
shone through her eyes, such vitality…
A husband old, jobless and a drunk,
half a dozen children hungry,
it would have the bravest spirit sunk...

Yet she laughed at destiny, her name,
the most cruel irony...
Self-pity wasn't her game.
She was an unsung hero,
who to the world was less than,
and to some probably considered a zero...
But to me she was an elevated soul, the best...
Oh Asha dear, you have earned your rest.

And the Angels cried

She was 5, a motherless child,
running around barefoot,
unsupervised.

He was her neighbour,
twenty at his prime...
A pedophile...

A predator on the prowl,
he found her an easy victim,
who couldn't cry foul.

He lured her like an unsuspecting prey,
fed the starving girl,
who hadn't eaten for a day...

He then lay her body down on the couch,
she was helpless, timid like a mouse...
as he devoured her innocence...
she tried to scream,
but could offer no resistance.

And the Angels in heaven cried...
They held her while she whimpered,
torn inside and outside...

Nobody believed her story,
to add insult to injury
and her deep misery.

Hushed clandestine whispers,
to protect his family from shame,
drove the little girl further into blinding pain.
She carries that weight around for posterity,
the irony...
He like an animal still prowls around,
his little victims,
silenced and buried in the ground.

Assumptions and Presumptions

The major obstacles in the roadmap of life,
are the stop signs that we have inside...
Most placed through error of judgment,
no rational basis, just figments of imagination.
Assumptions and presumptions fly around,
road blocks and misunderstandings surround.
When a situation we perceive,
we bring to it our inner beliefs...
Why can't we wipe the slate clean,
and from wisdom our response glean?
In communication with regular folk,
don't assume, presume and presuppose...
This leads to conflicts,
defensive behaviour and creating rifts,
through that quagmire, we must ourselves lift.
Instead introduce faith and love in your dealings,
people rise up to meet these feelings...
You will their misgivings dispel,
their qualms, misconceptions also quell.
Be quiet and listen to your body,
it's alarm system is never faulty...
If you do in your stomach feel weak,
a sense of misgiving, when to the stranger you speak...
Pay attention, it is an indication,
that something is not quite right,
in your interaction,

Silence picks up many messages,
which get lost in noisy reception...
Instead of the constant talk in our heads,
we should listen to our bodies instead.
Our creator has given us a perfect barometer,
in our bodies, to gauge external pressure,
so use the tools that you've been given,
rise above the presuppositions!

At the End of the Day

At the end of a long grueling day,
washing off the wonders, blunders and failures...
He felt elated, knowing that
Her sweetly perfumed, soft, loving and warm body...
Would be curled up in his arms.
All would be well in the world again!

Be Gentle with Yourself

Be gentle with yourself,
don't run, don't rush or try to keep pace...
it's life, you don't have to compete,
like a race.
Cherish all your strengths and weakness,
they make you complete,
and have their purpose...
Life is a journey of discovery...
it's for some, learning and recovery.
Let good intentions, light up your path,
the universe is kind, to those who are empaths.
Treat yourself like a long-lost friend,
enjoy your own company,
even though it isn't the trend...
within lies the true friendship of Self,
and it's fringe benefits, never end...
Love and pamper yourself,
don't wait for a lover or a friend...

It's nobody else's responsibility,
to amuse or delight you,
that is the stark reality.
The Self within you awaits,
visit it in silence,
your joy consummate!

Be Selective

Be selective of what you let into your space,
it can affect your mind and your peace erase.
Don't let negativity from the environment,
invade your thoughts and become a contaminant.
Stay away from prejudice and bias,
hatred and anger, all lead to crisis.
You have a duty to yourself,
to honour your being,
and in calmness dwell.
You are a carrier,
so create a barrier.
stay away from strife, and the mischief-makers.
Your purpose is too important,
to become redundant.
Protect yourself, immunize, sensitize,
purge the toxicity and danger imminent.
Choose your friends, work and leisure wisely,
it is not pride,
or considered impropriety.
You are responsible for your soul's sobriety,
Stay in the light, away from notoriety.
You have a standard that you have set,
don't go with the crowd, and those, who evil abet.
The folks who are beneficial for your soul,
will respect that,
and will keep you whole.
Those who don't, you need to let go,

in order for peace and serenity to flow.
Wish them well,
don't your soul sell.
Or you might find yourself in Hades' deepest well!
Don't allow evil in your vicinity,
it will corrode your heart with its toxicity.
Hold yourself and raise the bar high,
In order for you to with angel's fly!

Be You

Be you, everyone else is taken.
Don't be a version of someone else,
don't give in to others' shaming or coercion.
Don't worry about those who misunderstand you…
well-wishers won't be swayed by public opinion.
Your detractors and their myopic views,
can't comprehend, a beautiful, bold, spirit, that is true.

Free yourself of the need to please,
and the desire to masses appease.
Fools and their pre-conceived notions,
have poured into their views, poisonous potions…
You can't open a heart made of stone,
with all it's good sense and compassion foregone.

A frog thinks the whole world is his pond,
he cannot comprehend the magnificent universe beyond!

So live fearless, live big and true, be yourself…
Be unapologetically YOU!

Begin Again

You may think that it is all over,
don't give up,
begin again...

Look at the caterpillar,
when it did not give up,
it did transcend...

Life is not over,
you can still your life mend...
Look your challenges in the face,
don't let them drive you round the bend.

Don't ever give up,
begin again…
The show must go on,
until the end!

Beyond

Beyond the dark clouds of gloom,
beyond where fear does loom,
beyond the shroud of sorrow,
that does you adorn,
lies a seed of hope waiting to bloom.
Time and place are mere illusions,
relationships, possessions, creating blind confusion.

Look beyond with eyes of soul,
the life you live, is just a role...
Characters are cast in the play,
for you your virtues to display.
You have come from eternal light,
don't let sadness dim your spirit bright.

The love on earth that we experience.
will meet us again, beyond the realm of reason.
So be patient dear one, don't spiral into grief,
because your term on earth with love was brief.
Your love awaits you in another dimension,
you will meet again, this is but a brief intermission.

And when your time on earth is done,
you will frolic again with your love...
In another time—another sun.

Breath

How precious is the breath,
we inhale, exhale, and feel so refreshed…
With every breath pregnant possibilities,
endless potential with your innate abilities.
It is a sacred gift from the Lord above,
that he showers, with his bounty and love…
His divine mercy comes through every breath,
so why do we live our lives, with so much regret!
We take so much for granted.
Stop the raving and ranting…
If your breath stopped,
what good are your mansions…
your foolish vanity in its pretentious wrapping…
You would lie stone cold dead,
with your gratitude unsaid.
So fill your heart and lungs with joy…
exhale, inhale,
your breath enjoy!

Broken Mirror

She felt like a broken mirror,
cracked, disfigured, with lost fervour…
The broken pieces, crying for redemption…
A cry for help, not retribution.
Each piece a sad tale told,
shattered dreams and lost innocence, hope sold…
She prayed to be healed, her prayers answered,
and her new destiny was revealed…

Courage then paid a visit,
it transformed her soul like an alchemist.
With self-love she glued her brokenness together,
she regained her confidence and with all her
strength mustered.
She transformed into an eloquent bard,
whilst putting together her life's shards.
She created a mosaic masterpiece,
a thing of beauty, from the fear and emptiness…
Her heart is now, serene and in peace,
Her spirit now beautiful,
flies bold and free…

Can You Miss Someone You Never Met?

Is it possible to miss someone you never met...
Long for those deep, delicious conversations,
you had in your head...
Fantasize about their touch, or yearn to see them smile,
would walk the earth for them,
go the extra mile...

Your heart muses,
in a daytime reverie,
missing someone you have never seen...

Can you miss,
or does your mind dismiss,
what sets your heart afire,
and craves for longingly!

Childless

Everyone looked at them like they were freaks,
having a child, for some...
is a measure of virility,
isn't it just probability,
or is it a biological feat?

Is it him, is it her...
the whispers and stares, the continuous murmurs...
it was really nobody's business,
so to initiate a conversation, they wouldn't dare!

Her womb ached, to bring to fruition...
The passion of their loins,
a beautiful culmination.
But evolution was held at ransom.
they were childless,
the irony was... poignant.

They yearned for progeny,
but were deprived of the fruit of love by destiny...
Nature had played a wild card,
the childless couple, from her womb,
she did discard.
But creation can take various forms...
Creativity and nativity, evolution does perform.

They were childless, a situation so hapless!

Common Enchantment

She did not wait for moments of breakthrough inspiration,
in her daily life, she constantly found moments of common enchantment.
The way a baby smiled,
when she saw her mother.
The dogs barking at the sight of a stranger,
the sweetness and headiness of freshly brewed coffee,
the chewiness of delicious toffee.
The chit chat with friends and neighbours,
the outrageousness of obnoxious rumours.
The way day followed night,
and the stars shone bright to her delight...
These were the things,
that painted her world just right.
Every sight, smell and sound,
heightened her senses,
She had found magic, inspiration and pleasure,
in common enchantment.

Cyber Fantasy

Aching loneliness,
body dysmorphia...
Internet chat rooms,
creating mass hysteria...
Attractions, distractions,
fantasy rules...
Swapping stories, experiences,
playing the fool...
21st century modified hunting grounds...
Searching, scouring,
for "The one,"
the "holy grail"
that eludes some...
The ache, the longing
gnawing at the insides,
dire desperation,
racking Internet sites.
Trying to catch,
some fresh fish in the net,
breaking rules, on impulse,
trying to beat the rest...
Flirting, subtle innuendoes,
subliminal messages,
reaching crescendo...
cyber fantasy has some in its clutches,
it's like quick sand,
with deceptive highs and rushes!

Dance with the Universe

Everything in the universe has a vibrational frequency,
a constant flow of dynamic energy...
So when the Universe, calls on you to dance,
don't reject it like an undesirable suitor,
change your stance.
Do the polka, fox-trot and tango,
resist the urge to play Mozart's Requiem and dance solo...
Be enthusiastic with Vivaldi's Four Seasons
you won't invite in sorrow, that's the simple reason.
When situations are going upstream,
don't be a "debbie downer" and in sadness retreat...
even when stress and sorrow wears you down,
don't wear your gloom like a crown.
Change your vibrational frequency,
and attract positive energy...
You will be in tandem with the universe,
to take the lead in the dance, don't be adverse.
Be the DJ, blast those decibels,
dance with the stars in heaven...
Dance with the universe!

Death, I am not Happy with You

Death I am not happy with you,
I have a bone to pick,
we are in a feud.
You have chosen our very best,
couldn't you have waited,
why do you our faith test?

You came like a thief in the night,
and stole our dear one, from under our eyes...
You have not won this fight,
this is just an interlude,
our loved one,
lives forever in our hearts,
though out of our sight.

You are just a long sleep,
though you have brought us to our knees...
and our broken hearts inconsolably weep.

Our Maker promised us an eternity,
and that we will live beyond Death's agony.
There will be a blissful forever more,
Death, you will then, be shown the door!

Disillusioned

In the darkness,
she foraged for the truth,
which sometimes seemed so elusive.
In other moments,
it came forward with so much clarity.
Self-doubt and confusion,
muddied the waters,
creating disillusionment,
and non-acceptance of the present moment.
Was it ever possible to find it and hold on to it,
she wondered...
Or was she doomed to a lifetime of finding it and
losing it!

Does She Love You Like I Did?

Does she love you like I did?
So many years have passed,
our love cries out in vain.
Love lies decomposing, but its vestige remains.
I wonder what would have happened,
had I stayed through the heartache and pain.
Would love have lasted, or would we be insane!

Does she love you like I did?
Does she know what makes you tick,
we were together through sin and sick...
Does she know how you loved me,
and why we called it quits,
that sometimes love is not enough,
and separation befits.

I promised myself that I would let go,
of what didn't honour me and get on with life's show...
But on days like this, I reminisce,
I wonder, does she love you like I did...
And if she does, I can rest in peace,
that my love, she loves you like I did!

Don't

Don't, stay away from your love,
because of your ego....
Imagine a tomorrow, without them.
How would that feel? Empty! Is it worth it?
Will your ego then, make you happy?

Don't Chase After People

Don't chase after people,
maybe their term in your life has come to an end...
Don't be bitter,
but towards them love send...
For everything there is a season,
and maybe their hearts need to mend...
Let feelings of meanness and hatred transcend.
It takes two to tango and to feud,
don't get into messy entanglements,
and ego's subterfuge.
Look with eyes of source,
with compassion and kindness,
we need to heal the world,
and end all fighting and madness.
Leave people alone,
and give them their right to feel and be...
Not everything seems as we do see.
Love overcomes all,
and pride comes before a fall...
It isn't your job to be the fixer-upper of brawls.
If they are meant to be in your life,
nothing can keep them away...
Let go, let God, and chase the blues away.
Be like a lamp, giving light to all,
the lamp doesn't lose its incandescence...
It shines brightly,
summer, winter or fall.

Exquisite Paradox

When you give up obsessive desire,
of outcome, of all that you aspire...
You set into action, forces that conspire,
bringing to the fore,
your desire to your door...
and revel in the exquisite paradox and ire.
Letting go,
let's in...
Have you noticed this!
The exquisite paradox,
set in rhythm and sync...
The ultimate mystery,
from beyond,
a matter we should consider and deeply ponder on.
So let go,
and watch the mystery unfold...
A delight for the heart and soul to behold!

Flashback

She cried herself to sleep,
a little baby, not yet a week…
She wondered at the noise all around,
sadness and anger did her surround.

She didn't sign up for this she thought,
was this what life was all about…
Parents who hated one another,
she would report to God,
that they didn't love each other.

Was it her fault, the little infant wondered,
she wanted to crawl back into the womb of her mother.
She had a flashback from her reverie…
A life that birthed in misery!

Freedom of Speech

Freedom of speech is raising
a controversy world-wide,
It is an umbrella, that some use
their hatred to hide...
Remarks that are hurting and obviously snide,
should be avoided and thrown by the road-side.

Does freedom give you the right
to hurt one another?
Slander beliefs and abuse your brother?
You think you're smart and being so cool,
but it casts serious aspersions, that you are a fool.

It is wise instead to be sensitive,
to draw people together, rather than be divisive...
It requires intelligence to breach divides,
the way of the fool, is to spout rhetoric vile.

Use your speech wisely to heal hearts,
the tongue is a weapon, don't use it to throw
poisonous darts...
A world where we can all be at ease,
and leave a legacy of bliss and peace...
respect and tolerance, a hallmark to achieve,
I know its possible, that UTOPIA I perceive!

Gender Bender

Why does anybody have to tell him,
what he can, or cannot be...
he is stuck in a man's body,
but inside is trapped femininity.

There are some issues emerging,
clouding up some folks moralities,
creating confusion,
making them lose clarity...

They shun and cast aspersions,
on those struggling with gender identity...
making judgements on issues that are,
beyond the realm of their sensibilities.

It really is nobody's business,
about what gender some folks choose to be,
it's better than living their life as a lie,
and hiding their reality.

He has cried so many nights,
cross-dressing in secrecy,
wondering how to tell friends and family,
that the 'he' they see is in fact a 'she.'

He lives from moment to moment,
in pain and ambiguity...

The lines are not clear,
how your body identifies as a 'she.'

Let us as a society,
let up on these souls,
and of our judgements,
set them free!

To the issue of gender benders...
to love, compassion and empathy,
let your heart surrender!

Gone Without a Trace

All memories of life erased,
Gone without a trace...
Was it foul play,
a missing persons case...
Or a ploy, a ruse,
to an identity erase.
A person, who breathed,
loved, laughed, cried...
In a flash no more,
a ghost without a voice...
Vanished, disappeared, a life-long search...
for the girl who disappeared,
on a warm sunny day in March.
A family left behind with no closure,
was she kidnapped, murdered,
is her story over?
An open parentheses,
hanging overhead,
like the sword of Damocles...
Leaving behind hearts,
aching with heart-break,
diseased...
Gone without a trace,
all life's dreams defaced!

Grandma's House

Going to Grandma's house was always special…
Hugs and kisses, laughter and giggles…
Tasty treats that she would rustle up in a jiffy,
her arms and home, was so warm, full of love,
and oh so comfy.
Her beautiful eyes, would always light up…
Her gentle touch, her tone kind, never harsh or rough…
Grandma's house was a little piece of heaven,
a gift on this earthly realm, by the Almighty given!

Grief

When a loved one dies...
Sorrow envelopes, you scarce feel alive,
you desire nothing,
your soul can't sing.

Grief goes through stages,
first denial, then in storms and rages...
Some barely cope.
Hope dangles in a hangman's rope.
You sink into deep depression,
bargain with God for concessions...
When the anger subsides,
acceptance takes you to the other side.
You then feel a comforting presence,
as if your loved one is here, you sense their essence.
You cling to memories of old,
where you and your loved ones each other behold.

Take your time to grieve and heal,
your inside wounds may never seal...
Remember in the darkest night,
the stars shine the most bright.
The Lord is by your side,
your loved one in heaven resides.
Remember to gaze up at the sky
An angel you know therein abides.

Her Darkness

Darkness slithered
as a snake in the wild,
in the dead of night...
so grotesque, a fright.
She wondered from where it birthed,
how all her shameful secrets unearthed.
It touched her at the most sensitive...
Her flesh crawled, her fears inhibitive.
It slithered from groin through gut,
into her throat and out into the air it cut...
Shooting from visceral depths,
Into the world such virulence leapt!
With a guttural cry, she curled into a fetal ball...
Wishing she could die...

I Thank You

I thank you
for disappearing
without a forwarding address…
For a while, I was a hot mess…
and when my tears depleted…
I realized
I was enough.
My soul rejuvenated…
You are the real loser…
of a heart, devoted and sincere
and I, hit the jackpot
because you can't lose, what you have not…
I am happy now.
You taught me to be whole…
even though I lost my heart
I found my soul!

If We Could Live Our Lives Backwards

If we could live our lives backwards,
would we revisit the cemetery of lost love and broken dreams?
Would we opt for a different path?
Rethink unwise decisions made in the throes of wrath,
only to rue the reckless aftermath?
Or would we trust in the wisdom of consciousness that all that happened,
was not random chance,
but essential to the elevation of soul...

In My Lifetime

In my lifetime I've seen, sinners turn into saints...
and saints, tainted, full of disdain.
People turning their nickels and dimes,
into fortunes, rising high off the sweat and grime...
Folks living a life of crime,
walking around free, not serving time...
The innocents with necks to the yoke,
imprisoned in poverty and misfortune,
always broke.
Babies, the elderly and the sick are fair game,
war spares nobody,
not even the destitute or lame...
Brothers against brother, for a piece of land...
don't they know,
they will leave this world with nothing in hand...
There are no rules, nothing is sacred...
People washing their dirty linen, on the web, in public...
Banks and pharma, are big business...
trampling and feeding on the carcasses,
of all mankind without ethics.
Governments, no longer protecting the common man,
the rich are getting richer,
with the government, hand in hand...
In my lifetime I have seen,
so many things—horrid and obscene!

Inferno

Being in his presence,
drowning in his essence...
His cells spoke to hers,
in a language,
privy to only the two of them.
He made her come alive,
though sadness had cut through her heart like a knife...
It was like he knew,
the secret key to her heart...
and with his words,
he stoked the smoldering embers,
and made them come alive,
into a fiery, raging inferno,
burning everything around...

It Makes Me Sad

It makes me sad,
to see that most of us have become like robots...
mindlessly tiring from morning to night,
to pay bills...
a mortgage, put kids through school...
We go to work,
every day at the same time,
come home, make dinner,
run around to take children for activities.
And then go to bed,
tired and spent.
We have forgotten,
and have no time...
to laugh, talk to our neighbours,
play with our kids,
make love, read a good book,
get wet in the rain,
have a cup of coffee,
putting our feet up on the couch and listen to old records.
Sing out tunelessly when our song plays on the radio.

We just do the same things everyday...
day in, day out...
It makes me sad,
that we have lost our soul!

Just a Housewife

She wakes up at the crack of dawn
to prepare breakfast, without a word.
Tirelessly works behind the scenes.
Many a time, she stifles screams.
Washing, cleaning, preparing meals…
from dawn to dusk, soundlessly.
She is an unsung hero
though in her home
she feels her worth
is less than zero.
Her list of chores is endless,
she plays multiple roles,
attends to them with energy boundless…
She is the backbone of her home.
Just a housewife?
It's a denial syndrome!

Let Them Fly

We tend to be over-protective
towards our children,
we mean well,
but our actions, act like a deterrent...
It prevents their growth,
and real life education,
setting them up for failure,
stunting their intuition.

Once you have laid a good foundation
of values and life-lessons,
you have to give them the freedom...
To make choices,
good or bad,
without your condemnation...
Your job is to be a guide,
not a prison guard,
to contain them.

How will you build up their confidence,
if you second guess,
each and every one of their actions.
True love is letting them fly,
to experience highs and lows,
that life brings by.

Making mistakes and learning,
is what we are here for...
Not all of us are going to be unblemished,
or have a life of grandeur...
Some of us will stumble and fall,
and that is okay...
Let us help our children, truly stand tall!

Letters to My Children

Fill the earth with your laughter, love and caring,
don't be dismayed,
with folks that are hard and unwavering...
Be kind to those who need it most,
heed your soul's guidance,
when I'm gone...
Don't run from pillar to post.

Be the champion of the under-dog,
the beggar, the down-trodden,
the sick, the seniors
and those whose minds are in a fog...
Remember those that the world forgot,
bring a smile to their lips,
don't let their minds and bodies rot.

Remember to always wipe the tears,
of those whose hearts are breaking,
are weary and laden with burdens and fears...
Be passionate, compassionate,
not rude and obstinate,
even though that may be the trend.
Lend a helping hand,
to those that need a friend.

My darling children,
if you remember and follow this,
I can rest in peace, in happiness and bliss,
as you are my living legacy to the world,
I live through you,
In your actions and words...

Letting Go

Letting go of the shadows in my head,
Letting go of lost dreams, time to move ahead...
Letting go is like birthing in a new form,
Free of the prison of obsessive thoughts.
Resurrect—a soul reborn!
Release pent up emotion
that holds you back in everyday commotion...
release harmful energy,
rebuild a brand-new synergy.
Letting go, is the first step towards healing,
make peace with what it is, don't hit the ceiling...
Understand the lesson,
implement it with mind and reason...

Easier said than done?
but do you like where you are?
Time to change the status quo,
No time for subtle innuendoes.
Let go. Let go. Let God...

Loss

Sadness is akin to loss…
Loss of love, health, friendship, possessions…
we carry as a cross
and despair and gloom envision.

Consider for a moment
a new possibility
a new reality…
loss in the laws of duality
is but a portal for creativity.
A change of heart or bent of mind,
opens the channel for the plan divine.
Something that human comprehension,
may not fathom in the higher dimension.
Observe nature, when hit by calamity,
does not resist but adjusts to the new reality…
Flexibility is the key,
to see what the mind cannot readily see.

Loss peels off the layers of superficiality
and we, raw and ready,
with heart and mind a worthy crucible
for the divine to enter a domain now venerable.

Every time loss strikes
good will come from it,
trust your Lord to make it right!

Minefields

Navigating the minefields of her life,
she still found the courage,
to sow seeds
of kindness and love...

Who knew
that from so much ugliness,
such beautiful flowers would grow!

Misfit

She never felt like she belonged anywhere.
She always felt so lonely, even in a crowd.
Something always stirred in her heart,
a kind of beckoning to worlds unknown.
Prompting her to take a different path,
from the known and familiar,
making her a Misfit, an oddity,
amongst her peers.
She tried to go through the motions of a normal
life, with stoicism.
But she always felt an unease.
Not superior or inferior,
but different and so alone!
A Misfit!

My Heart Lies in Mumbai

My heart lies in Mumbai,
in little gallis, eating usal,
sipping garma garm Chai...
Gobbling wada pav and kachori,
calling elders unrelated, Uncle and Aunty!

The familiar sights and sounds of home,
the market lingo,
bargaining with vegetable and fish vendors at the
door...
I miss the familiar streets...
urchins, astrologers,
stray dogs and cats of different breeds.

Sitting in rickshaws,
wind blowing through my hair,
eating in roadside dhabas,
amidst everybody's stares
The warmth and love of neighbours and friends,
the endless adventures,
that we thought,
would never end.

My heart lies in Mumbai,
the city that never sleeps,
the apple of my eye!

Not Missed

She didn't show up to work,
she was not missed.
She couldn't pay her rent,
her life had fallen to pieces.

A nondescript, forgotten soul,
whose life was amiss.
Nobody cared about her,
as she wasn't rich,
beautiful or talented.
Her friends were more like acquaintances,
she had no meaningful alliances…

She was just a sorry, sad, soul,
nobody loved her.
She just crawled into a sidewalk hole…

Hid herself from the hurtful stares,
the truth of the matter is nobody cares!
She was not missed, homeless, just a statistic!

Ode to Curry

Curry days,
spice ingrained,
in my DNA,
forever to stay...
Vegetables, chicken and goat...
stewed in a tasty base,
curry is my favorite taste...
Coming together in my mouth,
exploding across my taste buds,
rocking my world...
My identity,
a throwback to my ancestry.
Coriander and cumin,
fraternizing with,
garam masala, chillies and curcumin...
Blended together aromatically,
to titillate the palate,
enticingly.
Oh curry,
you have raised the culinary bar,
across the board,
you are the most delicious,
by far!

Old Pictures

Looking into the box of old pictures,
she picks up one, frayed at the edges.
All that was left of passion's storms...
A faded photo memory.
How happy they looked together...
Not knowing that the future held such irony.
And one day the ecstasy that they felt,
would lie at the bottom of an old box of pictures,
forgotten and buried.

On the Subway

On the subway home from work,
I look at the faces around me, a sea of humanity...
Each with a different story to tell,
some lives of joy, some a living hell.
What if our thoughts and life experiences,
were visible like the lines on our faces,
would we then towards each other,
show love and care and be more amiable?

Practice

In the face of adversity,
practice resilience...
In the face of hardship,
practice endurance.
In the face of loss,
practice patience.
In the face of tragedy,
practice courage.
In bad times,
practice hope,
In good times,
practice humility.
In all times practice equanimity.

In desperate times,
keep your sanity.
In sad times
practice cheerfulness.
In times of need,
practice thrift.
In times of plenty,
generosity.
In times of boredom,
curiosity.

In the best of times, in the worst of times.
practice being yourself!

Prisoner of My Mind

I was a prisoner of my mind,
when I lived in the past,
and did old memories rewind...
My two jailors,
fear and doubt...
Filled me with unease,
and sorrow brought.
They hovered around my every thought,
resulting in disappointments and self-doubt...
They pulled their veil over my eyes,
that kept me away from the light.
When I reached rock-bottom I had a choice,
to plunge further into darkness,
or save myself and change my plight...
I prayed to God for courage to fight...
old demons that reared from my thoughts,
And kept me from the light...
By, God's grace, I arose,
like a Phoenix from the ashes,
and turned to self-love,
the sweetest smelling rose.
My journey into self-awareness my jailors upset,
they tried old settings to reset...
They soon realized their wiles imminent,
were no longer permanent.
With prayer, hard work and meditation,
I changed my path and destination...

It was a difficult journey to self-purification…
weeding out doubts and self-recrimination.
It called for courage and brutal honesty,
to make room for pure integrity.
I am grateful for the journey I undertook,
of self-awareness,
for which all pretenses I forsook...
Bringing me to the other side,
where my true self lies,
with love and arms open wide!

Progeny

Nature conspired with Destiny,
and concocted a time-tested recipe.
They took some part of you,
and some part of me,
and created our delightful progeny...

They cautioned us with some advice,
don't try to save them from sadness, despair or vice...
You see they have come to earth to just BE...
and experience an exciting destiny.

What may seem like misfortune,
is a learning curve,
let them experience it with abandonment and verve,
You are their guide, not their serf,
watch and delight,
whilst their souls' lessons learn...

I know it can be trying and hard,
trust in the Lord,
He has this covered.
He will keep them in his loving hands you see,
for we are all his progeny!

Pump Up Your Faith

Pump up your faith,
decrease your speed...
don't live life in overdrive,
be at ease.
Life can be a joyride,
if you believe...
don't anticipate problems.
Many gifts you will receive!

Faith can move mountains,
as you have often heard...
It is not mumbo jumbo,
or talk absurd.

Give it a shot,
what do you have to lose...
Your dreams await you,
with worry sign a truce!

Raw

Jagged nerves,
feelings exposed…
On edge,
logic with emotion,
juxtaposed.
Does he? Does he not?
Questions continuously play in my head…
I take unfulfilled desires
like thorns to my bed…
A communication disconnect,
emotions unread…
passion unfed…
Tantalizing. Alone…
I wonder,
could it be had raw,
and my heart not be torn?

Refugee

He came from a foreign land,
displaced, robbed of his life,
terror gripping his motherland.
Death lurked on every street,
he had no safe place to retreat…
Refugee status,
alien country,
strange tongue and customs,
a small price to pay to be free…
Past erased,
a new identity embraced…
His pulse races,
will they accept him?
He struggles to let hope surface!

Rise Above Judgment

What you look at, and react to in others,
is also in you...
Your world mirrors your inner reality,
and reflects the truth...
The annoyance you feel
at imagined hurts that you conceal,
if you the layers of your soul unpeel,
you will see what makes you so feel.
When you to the unconsciousness in others, don't
react...
From wisdom and higher consciousness
you will your response extract.
The words in the Bible
"why do you see the speck in your brother's eye,
and fail to see the beam in your own"
demonstrates the fact...
That what we see in others is often in ourselves,
so rise above judgment,
and your highest self reflect...

Soulfie

A tidal wave of selfies,
drowning us all in external superficialities.
Bodies are shells to house humanity,
isn't it ironical we flaunt that to the gallery?

Going deeper than the superficial,
avoiding the hype of this social ritual.
Why the fake appearance,
when the soul is pure and ageless.

Be bold, break the boundaries
of mindless social quandaries.
Trying to fit in, belong in society
is an exercise in total futility.
Mankind was always meant
to express diversity.
It is time for authenticity
Set the soul free!
Take a soulfie!

Sex Sold

Sex sold… brazenly.
Hot sultry summer,
each dancing to the tune of their own drummer.
Micro-minis, mid-riffs bare,
hips doing a shimmy, in all weather.
Warm breeze, all season tease…
Ankle bells, heightened sensuality sells.
Women young and old,
by sugar daddies to the highest bidder sold.
Cheap perfume, stereo blaring,
men in cars cruising, at the women hungrily staring…
Humanity at its lowest ebb,
Greed and addiction, degradation and desperation spread.
Exploitation, slavery in another form,
the human spirit, debased and deformed.
Sex and depravity, slickly packaged together…
dreams and innocence, in the gutter.

She Bled Quietly

She bled quietly, stoically.
Through the gash in her heart...
Made by the knife of cruelty
that many had thrust deep…
some with ferocity,
others tempered by their weaknesses...
Each left indelible imprints,
like dirty feet on pristine soul.
The deepest, the most unkind,
was the one he had made,
with no regrets,
just vanishing into the night,
without a goodbye.
Like a phantom.
Was it a dream, or was it reality?
She began to doubt her sanity.
She bled quietly...

She Dreamed of Being a Princess

She dreamed of being a princess,
but became a witch instead...
In the tomb of her innocence,
her naiveté lay dead...

Her prince charming she wished,
she had never kissed...
A toad in disguise,
the irony not hard to miss.

Cruel life robbed her of throne and crown,
a life of drudgery,
became her lot.
Over time the princess transformed into a witch.
Unable was she to stop the switch.

No fairytale ending,
curtains drawn...
The corpse of the princess,
lay on bare ground...
From the ashes emerged the gnarled witch,
in the fairy tale, there was a glitch!

She Stood her Ground

She picked up all the hurtful things
her tormentors had said to her,
glued them together with firm resolve.
'A work in progress,' she called herself.
She then arose like a Phoenix from the ashes
The ruins of a tumultuous life.
Prostrated in the temple she had erected,
shunning the idols that once controlled her.
She transformed into a goddess of self-love.
Ironically—her devotees were the same ones
who had viciously slandered her.
They came to stare and flatter.
Fickle as the wind.
She stood tall and regal,
neither flattery nor criticism could topple her
crown.
She smiled with grace. She stood her ground.

Silence

How is beauty created?
In silence...
Creativity tiptoes in the valley of silence,
guiding spirit in divine creation.
Silence allows desire to manifest.
Welcome it into your heart,
for a mystical experience.

Silence in divine orchestration,
leads soul and skill to creative dance.
Invite silence like a lover, for a secret rendezvous...
embrace it and let it
bring out the best in you.

Sitting at My Window

Sitting at my window, watching the world go by,
friends sometimes stopping to say hi...
Looking curiously at passers-by, a game I play,
to guess what goes on in their lives,
by looking deep into their eyes.
Some rushing home, some strolling all alone…
Little girls playing hopscotch on the street,
Lads cycling around at full speed…
Babies expressing themselves,
with laughter, gurgling or shrieks.
The old, the young, married, single,
sometimes a nun or a priest.
Vendors selling their wares on the street,
housewives gossiping, when they meet…
Life happening, while I sit,
on my little window seat...
It is such a wonderful past-time,
a daily treat!

Slow Death

She watched the clock tick...
Familiar sounds in the house,
children crying next door,
husband and wife arguing over the sound of the telly...
Doors slamming shut,
teenage drama,
radio blaring out the latest tunes...
Today's news,
bland and insipid.
Monotony,
ad nauseam...
She craved unpredictability.

Slow death,
like the spider on the wall,
spinning a web,
catching the fly
that inevitably
came by.

So What?

So what if they don't like you?!
You like yourself, and that's enough!
Don't let them get to you.

So what if they misunderstand and misquote you,
some are bent on doing so.
At least you know where they stand.
Don't let their tricks fool you.

So what if you stand your ground,
you were meant to live large,
and not by the obsolete bound.

So what if you are sometimes alone?
You complete you! Enough as a stand-alone.
So what if you speak your mind?
Be true to yourself, and not herd blind.

So what if you made mistakes?
There is always an opportunity for retakes.
So what, if you haven't figured life out...
life doesn't always clues give out.

Don't live life playing to the gallery.
Be the anomaly!
So what?!!

Sorry to Disappoint You

Sorry to disappoint you,
I am not who I was yesterday…
I will not be caught in a time warp,
till I am old and grey.
I am no longer the person you knew.
Inconsistent? No!
Learning and experience change one's view.
Hell no! I will not be yesterday's stale news…
So, if you are nostalgic,
for the girl you once knew,
sorry to disappoint you,
I wasn't put on earth to please you.
Let me introduce my new self to you.
A self that has outgrown the old self-doubt,
now strong like an oak,
with branches of wisdom spread out…
A self that has weathered many storms,
and with a new resilience been reborn.
So, sorry to disappoint you,
the little girl you once knew,
is now a strong woman,
with spirit renewed.

Stay With Me

Stay with me,
till the dawn brings new hope,
with the sun's early rays, our love will be reborn.
I didn't think that it would come to this,
I thought our love would weather every storm.
Weren't you the one who swore to love me forever?
Who lies dead?
Love... Or you my love?
Stay with me!

Stress

The curse of these times is stress,
causing physical and mental breakdowns,
our endurance does test.
We are in constant pressure,
to perform, produce...
We have lost our pleasure,
we have our enjoyment reduced.
Competition has raised its evil head,
making us go at each other's throats,
our lives are a mess...
Relaxation and enjoyment are like bad words...
we are ashamed to enjoy life,
it is an offense,
and a thought absurd.
Do better,
work harder is the mantra,
stress is the gladiator in the arena.
Stress is the leading cause of death and disease,
it ruins our lives and fills us with unease…
we can no longer do as we please,
we are the prisoners of stress, begging for release.
Mankind has lost its way,
stress is running our lives,
and is here to stay!

Suicide

She felt so dead inside,
life seemed empty and meaningless...
She found no joy,
in day to day situations.
The worm of depression,
was eating her up inside,
she wanted to crawl up in bed and hide.

Conversation, daily routine, she didn't want,
how do you explain that to the world?
That living has lost its charm.
Day to day activities,
such draining tasks,
it took every shred of willpower not to fall apart.

Addiction, job loss, divorce—a process,
that made her spiral into a bottomless abyss.
She died a little every day,
and had totally lost her way.
She felt so alone in an unfriendly world,
She wouldn't be missed—her last words.

As the noose tightened,
she felt the pain of death.
Sadly, even then
there was no regret.

The Ache

I reached into the ache
in my soul,
to gently palpate...
Sorrow, lost dreams struggled out,
ghosts, shadows, I had learned to live without.

Each a clue to unravel and use...
The ache begets
the passion, the longing, the calling –
our creative bequests.

From the ache my true self emerged,
stronger, when I my soul purged...
Go deep into the ache,
and all of its mysteries partake!

The Beggar

He sat at the far corner of the street,
under the lamplight,
his tattered blanket,
barely covering his feet...

His face lined with defeat.
Life had dealt him a difficult hand,
a cripple from birth, he gave up,
and hid his sagging faith in the sand...
The pariah dog was his best friend,
fate had joined their spirits, together to mend.

Both outcasts of society,
fallen from grace, together in adversity.
Man and his best friend, resemble each other...
Irony did not spare them,
in perverse humour.

Both lay covered from head to toe with sores...
They were comrades in arms,
in every sense of the word.
Each night the dog lay in his arms.
The beggar and his friend with a bowl for alms.

The Bus Journey

The bus rattled on, putrid smoke rising,
fellow travelers asleep...
She smiled, snug and smug
her fingers interlaced with his.
She lost all sense of time,
all she knew was contentment,
now that they were together.
Every moment with him,
was sweet pleasure and magical.
The long, difficult journey to their destination,
which many complained about...
She strangely savoured
because she was with him,
nothing else mattered.
Looking at him, she smiled..
He was perfect!
The city smells, acrid smoke rising
from burning wood stoves,
and clouds of toxic fumes
from the factories around...
Lay thick and eerily like
a filthy blanket wrapping the town.
Dirty garbage, piled up all around,
millions of flies, swooping giddily...
The stench of poverty and a tired humanity...
She squeezed his hand,
he smiled and she was transported...

The Dance

The eternal dance of souls in the cosmos...
Coming together,
Symbiosis... Drifting apart... Broken pieces... of their hearts.
Picked up by the next partner... patterns repeated.
Sometimes flowing in rhythm, culminating in rapture and ecstasy.
Other times erratic, disjointed, causing pain, disillusionment and agony.
Separation... Spinning out of control.
Collision with another soul on the same path.
The dance begins all over again.

The Flower

Her fragrance so intoxicating...
Her essence exquisite.
But not all drew close,
to appreciate it...
And those who did,
were inspired to create verse and art.
She was unaware of her beauty...
Would that she could look at herself,
through the eyes,
of those who loved her.

The Garden of the Soul

Plant the seeds of love in your heart,
watch them grow into trees of compassion…
Branches reaching out to all include,
even giving shade to the unkind and rude.
A tree never discriminates,
she gives abundantly,
even to those that hate…
Weed out your rigidity,
fertilize your soul with flexibility…
Watch your garden as it grows,
with rows and rows of friends not foes.
Remember to always pare and prune,
unwanted judgments as it will ruin,
the purity of your inner space,
and it will your soul abase…
Be mindful…
of the garden of your soul…

The Hunter and the Hunted

She hunted in the forest,
looking for her perfect prey.
One who would lie docile,
and let her have her way…
But she soon grew bored,
and wanted a challenge…
Or even to play a different role,
the hunted, without an advantage.
The rules of the game,
didn't change, she realized,
she was inside the same…
The hunter and the hunted,
lay wrapped up inside her,
it was insane…
She left the forest disenchanted,
happiness had eluded her again,
she went to bed, cleared her head…
and the most sublime thoughts,
in her heart were bred…
The hunter and the hunted,
were all inside of her…
she didn't need to pursue,
or be pursued to find what had escaped her…
She opened her heart to all life's experiences…
and basked in the freedom of being alone,
she wouldn't need to hunt or be hunted,
to feel happy and satisfied again.

The Little Girl Inside

I unleashed the little girl inside,
and set her free…
reminisced about days gone by,
over a cup of tea…
We laughed and talked till the crack of dawn,
giggling and cackling over secrets sworn.

I walked with her barefoot in the park,
not caring about the curious glances of strangers,
it in fact our mischievousness sparked.
We agreed it was indeed a sin,
to curb the inner child, and hold it all in…

There is no fun in being staid and serious,
dance like nobody is watching,
be spontaneous…
To the naysayers,
remain impervious.
I told her how much I loved her, no matter what
she had done…
Her eyes lit up,
she shone bright like the sun…

Now she and me,
we are one entity…
Together for all eternity!

The Old Itch

The old itch, twitched every now and then...
She scratched, it oozed
painful and purulent memories.
Time set a scab...self-protection.
But every now and then,
a memory would set off
the old itch.

The Shirt

His shirt lay crumpled on a chair forlorn,
it's owner now a pile of ashes in an urn.
She picked it up trying to recapture his scent,
was this what life comes to,
in the end?
She tried to trace the muscles of his chest from memory,
the shirt held bound in its threads,
yesteryears, birthdays and anniversaries...
How could the shirt that once held a man she loved,
so full of life.
Now lie crumpled, crushed, apologetic,
urging sad reminiscence...

She started to cry,
asking God why,
why did He take her love,
why did he have to die?

The shirt held in her hands
seemed so vacant,
like her heart,
limp and forlorn
whispering
'I'm innocent.'

The Trial

Hawk-eyed prosecutors circling their prey,
the Defendant,
innocent until proven guilty, will have his say.
The criminal justice system,
fraught with error,
letting go of crooks,
with brilliant lawyers unleashing terror.
The innocent so often receive a harsh sentence…
The law is flawed,
its cracks obvious to those with wisdom.

Court clerks at their typewriters
Clickety-click,
jurors sometimes out of deliberations,
faster than a wink.
Lawyers presenting and defending their stance.
The judge in the courtroom silence demands.
The courtroom has a deathly quiet,
when the jury comes in,
will he be proved guilty or will he be given respite?
A life will be sentenced in the flash of an eye,
will justice reign or will evil be let loose to fly?

The Unicorn, the Fairy, the Mermaid, the Clown

Washed onto the shore
were parts of her childhood.
The unicorn, the fairy, the mermaid, the clown.
Lost innocence trampled by many to the ground.
Sharks then took charge, claiming ownership...
Nobody threw a lifeline to save her.
Was this how it would go down?
She wrote to ease the pain,
and to her senses regain.
Giving her release, into her childhood domain.
Of unicorns, fairies, mermaids, clowns...
A world where she could forever remain.

Today

Today,
I woke up.
Made a to-do list...
Embraced the interruptions,
that came along the way.
Realizing,
that life has its own tempo and
agenda...
With irreverent contempt,
for to-do lists and inertia.
A momentum,
to gauge and play along.
With or without you,
life's melody plays on...
Today and everyday!

You are Beautiful

You are beautiful,
you are enough…
In your heart lies the strength…
never give up!
Look right back in the eyes
of your tormentors who say,
you are unworthy and
wished you weren't this way..
The Master created you,
with a brilliant stroke of his brush…
How could you ever not be enough…
You are beautiful!

Vigilant

Teddy bear lying on the driveway,
child kidnapped, heading for the highway.
Amber alert, description of vehicle and child,
heart-rending pleas,
to bring the child back alive...

Predators lying in every corner,
you cannot even trust your next-door neighbour...
A child can be taken from the street or school...
Street-proofing kids, at school and home,
is now the unwritten rule.

Child-trafficking is on the rise,
take good care of your kids,
be vigilant, be wise.

Walls

Most of us greet and interact with each other,
with invisible walls erected between us.
Some walls were built in self-defense,
and years of being betrayed or let down,
by those we have loved and lost.
Some walls have been built,
because of a false sense of superiority,
thinking that we are better than the rest.
Both create separation,
and lead to unhappiness...
It takes courage, strength and deep soul-searching,
to bring down those walls,
and trust and love again,
unreservedly.

War

No good has ever come from war,
both the conquered and the conqueror,
suffer loss of lives, property... live in fear.
The aftermath of war is death and destruction,
causing sorrow, complete ruination.
War is a devious activity,
promulgated by politicians and the arms industry...
to create markets for weapons proliferation,
profiting from death...
greed and lust for power, their motivation.
Fueling fear and creating controversy,
making grounds for aggression.
Instead of using diplomacy and peaceful resolution.
There is nothing that cannot be resolved by healthy communication!
Lives bartered for greed,
will we not the cries
of the orphaned children heed!

We are all One

When will we realize that we are all one?
Diversity, for variety...
An exercise, by the universe,
to breed tolerance, not hostility.
Let's think of ourselves as part of one body...
If the hand hurts,
the head feels it...
We all share the same parentage...
Adam and Eve, our father and mother...
So why can't we love each other,
like sisters and brothers?

What am I?

What am I?
Am I just a melting pot of flesh and blood,
thoughts and feelings,
in a memory flood…
A cocktail of DNA,
a cultural pool,
a cosmic tool?
Am I this body,
that goes through many stages,
or the mind, the CPU,
that the whole mechanism manages?
Or the soul,
that acts like a compass,
to give good conscience,
to the masses…
I cannot be only a body…
something impermanent,
so filled with impediments…
or only the mind,
mercurial and unstable…
Or the soul,
what happens to those, without a conscience or
directionless?
Do they just have a big gaping hole
instead of a soul?
And then when all goes,
Am I to presuppose,

that my body, mind and soul,
will be shut in a vault,
till judgment day,
decides my final repose?
Or am I a force,
that pulses,
through all life,
and all its faces...
Animate, inanimate,
it does all my theories and fallacies shatter...
The life force that exists,
beyond matter?
The force that mischievously takes different shapes and forms,
rendezvous with matter and watches it perform...
And when I am no longer here,
where will this force then reappear,
or will I then forever disappear!

Wouldn't You Rather Just be Ordinary?

Is it wrong to wish for the ordinary?
No high jinx,
but a life uneventful
to the point of monotony.
The day to day, plodding on.
The desire for recognition
and glory foregone.

Existence flat-lining
on a comfortable plateau,
just even-keeled, no highs or lows.
An ordinary life,
with an ordinary husband or wife.
No cause for angst,
recriminations or strife.

No striving for extraordinary achievement,
content with ease and appeasement.
A life well lived
in the perimeter of the ordinary,
free from the stress
of proving one's abilities.
Creating an inner climate
of desperation and
anxiety.

Genius pays a heavy price,
walking the line of brilliance and insanity.
Mental illness has plagued
the great minds of humanity.

Wouldn't you rather just be ordinary,
and enjoy the joys of normalcy.
Satan with all his brilliance,
lies in the denizens of hell,
with all his over-achieving minions.

Wouldn't you rather be just ordinary?

Acknowledgements

To my husband, Nasser, my friend and companion for three decades, goes my gratitude for giving me the encouragement to follow my dreams. Thank you for the tolerance you had with my many bouts of creativity at all odd hours of the day and night.

I am thankful to my children, Yosha, Yohannah, Juwairiya, Ukasha and Aliya, who have been my cheerleaders, inspiration and motivation. You occupy the most special place in my heart.

Thank you to my parents, Alice and Robert Sequeira, my beacons of guidance and support, who always believed in me even in my turbulent teenage years. I know that this book will vindicate all those sacrifices you have made. Words are never enough to express my gratitude.

To Cheryl Antao-Xavier, my editor and publisher who plucked me from obscurity, I offer my sincere thanks. She has advised, cajoled and creatively criticized my many false starts and final drafts. Thank you for your wisdom, your kindness, your good nature, your patience and the many hours you have spent working with me. I am forever grateful for everything you've done.

My special thanks to my daughter, Yosha Khan, for designing the book cover at such short notice. You are a talent to reckon with and my rock. I am forever grateful.

To my Facebook family who has been patient with the many previews of my poems and gave me the courage to bring this project to fruition I offer my sincere thanks.

www.ingramcontent.com/pod-product-compliance
Lightning Source LLC
Chambersburg PA
CBHW071530080526
44588CB00011B/1621